Table Tennis

Heinemann
LIBRARY

First published in Great Britain by Heinemann Library,
Halley Court, Jordan Hill, Oxford OX2 8EJ,
a division of Reed Educational & Professional Publishing Ltd.

02 01 00 99 98
10 9 8 7 6 5 4 3 2 1

Series cover and text design by Karen Young
Paged by Jo Pritchard
Cover by Smarty-pants Design
Edited by Jane Pearson
Illustrations by Xiangyi Mo
Production by Alexandra Tannock
Printed in Hong Kong by Wing King Tong

ISBN 0431 08506 4

British Library
Cataloguing in Publication data:

Blackall, Bernie.
    Table tennis. – (Top sport)
    1. Table tennis – Juvenile literature.
    I. Title
    796.3'46

This title is also available in hardback edition ISBN 0431 08501 3.

Acknowledgements
The publisher would like to thank:
Rebel Sport, Prahran; students from Armadale Primary School –
Robert Klein, Nicola Murdock, Khoa Nguyen, Mimosa Rizzo,
Andrew Scott, Charlotte Sheck-Shaw and Zheng Yu; and Table
Tennis Australia

Special thanks to Glenn Tepper, National Coaching Director and
Oceania Development Officer, Table Tennis Australia, and to Fred
Martin and Pat Archdale for their assistance in the preparation of
this book.

Photographs supplied by:
Table Tennis Australia; Malcolm Cross, page 13; Empics pages 6, 7
State Library of New South Wales page 8.

Contents

About table tennis

Table tennis, sometimes known as ping pong, is a racket and ball game for two players (**singles**) or for four players (**doubles**). The table tennis racket is often called a bat.

The players hit a small light ball across a table which is divided by a low net. Each player aims to win points by playing shots that his or her opponent will be unable to return. If a player misses a shot, hits the ball into the net or off the table, or breaks a rule, a point is added to the opponent's score. The first player (or pair) to reach 21 points, with a lead of at least two points is the winner of the game. A table tennis **match** consists of three or five **games**.

Table tennis is a very popular sport with an estimated 22.5 million registered competitive players world-wide; it is second only to soccer as the world's most played sport. There are competitions for men and women, in singles and doubles and also mixed doubles. There are junior competitions for similar events.

Table tennis has been included in the Olympic Games since 1988.

Table tennis in China

Table tennis is China's national sport – there are more than 20 million registered players in China. Each national championship takes a year to complete and involves about one million players.

British champions

The first champions

The first table tennis championships were held in Crystal Palace, London in 1903. There was a prize of £25 for both the mens' and the womens' champions. This was a big prize for those days! The first English closed championships were held in 1921. The English closed is for English players only. Players from any country can enter an open championship.

World champions

England has had some world table tennis champions, but not for a very long time. Fred Perry is better known for playing tennis, but he was also the world table tennis singles champion in 1929. In the 1930s, Viktor Barna who was born in Hungary won the world singles championships five times, twice playing for England. He also won 14 other world titles. Richard Bergmann from Austria also played for England. The last English world singles champion was Johnny Leach who won twice, in 1949 and 1951. The twin sisters Diane and Rosalind Rowe were the world ladies doubles champions every year from 1948 to 1954.

Jill Parker, star player and coach

Jill Parker won the English closed championships seven times and the European ladies singles championships in 1975. She played doubles with Linda Howard in the same year and they became European ladies doubles champions.

Jill Parker, now a leading table tennis coach who helps the England women players of today.

Desmond Douglas
in action.

Desmond Douglas, record breaker

Desmond Douglas has never been world champion, but he has won more English titles than any other player. He was born in Jamaica in the West Indies but came to England as a child. He has won the English closed singles championships 11 times. Playing with partners, he has also won the mens' doubles 11 times and the mixed doubles 4 times. He is no longer England's number one player, but his fast attacking game and lightning reactions have always been exciting to watch.

Matthew Syed

England's current number one is 26-year-old Matthew Syed, who won the English National Championship and the Commonwealth Championship earlier this year.

Matthew Syed at the European Olympic qualifying competition, Manchester.

History of table tennis

Table tennis developed from a miniature version of real tennis. No one is sure of just when and where the game began, but it is thought that the first game took place in Wimbledon, England in the late 1800s. It was played on a table with a light ball and small bats.

Early table tennis bats were made of dried animal skin stretched across light wooden frames.

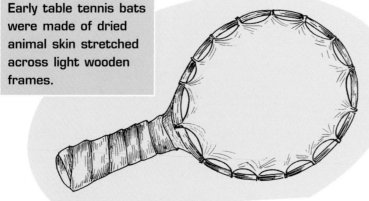

In the early 1900s table tennis gained world-wide popularity as an entertaining after-dinner pastime, but the craze was relatively short-lived. Then in 1926 the International Table Tennis Federation (ITTF) was founded. It aimed to promote and improve the game. Later that year, in London, the first World Championships were held. Between 1927 and 1939 competitions were dominated by Europeans. By the early 1950s Asian players were at the forefront of international table tennis.

By the 1940s table tennis was a popular game with both adults and children.

Rules

Before play starts

In competitions, a coin is tossed to decide which player will **serve** first and which end of the table each player will play from. The player who wins the toss can take the choice of serve or the choice of ends. The opponent will have the other choice. Players stay at the same ends for the whole of each game, except in the deciding game, where players change ends when the first player reaches 10.

Serving

The ball must be thrown up from a flat palm and hit from behind and above the end of the table. It must bounce on your half of the table, and then travel over the net to bounce on your opponent's half of the table. If the ball touches the net, but still travels over it to bounce on the other side, the serve is taken again.

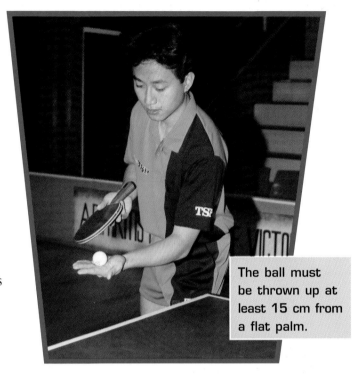

The ball must be thrown up at least 15 cm from a flat palm.

Doubles serving

When playing doubles, you must serve the ball so that it bounces on your half of the table on the right-hand side, and then travels across the net to bounce on your opponent's half of the table on the diagonally opposite side.

A correct serve. The ball is hit down so that it bounces on your side of the net before travelling across to your opponent's side of the table.

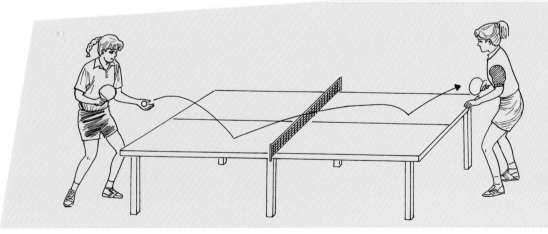

Rules

Continuing play

Once the ball has been served, players hit it back and forth until a player misses the ball or breaks a rule. Then a point is given to the other player and the next serve is taken. Players take turns to serve, changing each time five points have been scored, that is when the total number of points scored is 5, 10, 15, 20... If the score reaches 20–20, players have one serve each alternately.

You must hit the ball after it bounces once on your side of the table. You must hit it over the net so that it bounces on your opponent's half of the table.

Once the ball has bounced, you must hit it back across the net without it bouncing again on your half of the table.

A **point** is scored when your opponent:
- Misses the ball
- Hits the ball off the table
- Hits the ball into the net
- Hits the ball so that it bounces on his or her half of the table before going over the net
- Hits the ball while it is over the table but before it has bounced
- Allows the ball to bounce more than once before hitting it
- Hits the ball over the net and off the table without it bouncing
- Hits the ball so that it bounces on the side rather than the top surface of the table
- Makes an illegal serve
- Touches the table with his or her free hand.

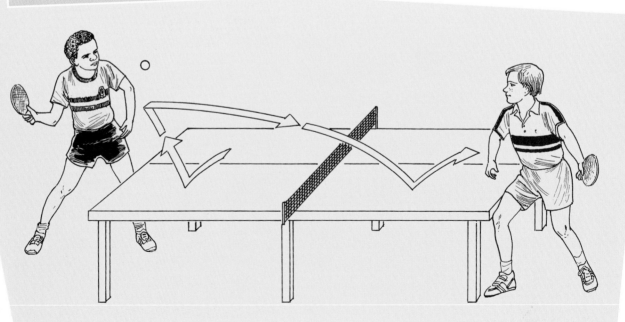

The server's total is always announced first. A score of 2–1 indicates that the player serving has scored 2 points, and her opponent has scored 1 point.

Scoring

A table tennis match consists of the best of three or five **games,** depending on the competition. A game is won by the player whose score reaches 21 points first. If the scores reach 20–20, a clear lead of two points is required to decide the winner. Players change ends after each game. In the last game, players change ends as soon as one player reaches 10 points.

The first player to win two games in a best of three games match, or three games in a best of five games match, is the winner.

Doubles

In doubles table tennis, partners take it in turns to hit the ball. At no time are you permitted to hit two consecutive shots.

Serving order for doubles

When it is your turn, serve five times from the right-hand corner of the table, diagonally across the table. One member of your opponents' team will receive all five serves. Then swap sides with your partner and he or she will receive the next five serves from your opponents.

When the ball is returned, the boy must play the next shot. If the girl hits the next shot, play will stop and a point will be awarded to their opponents.

What you need to play

The table

The table can be made of any material as long as the playing surface is not shiny. It is a dark colour (usually dark blue or green) with white lines marked around the edge and down the centre.

The table is about 2.7 metres long, 1.5 metres wide, and 0.75 metres high. The net is 15.25 centimetres high.

Players need plenty of space to move around the table. It should be positioned in an area at least 6 metres by 3.5 metres.

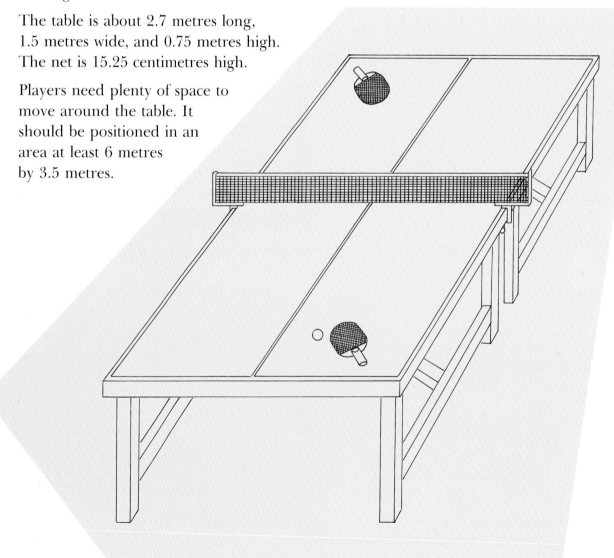

The ball

The ball is hollow and very light. It is made from white, yellow or orange celluloid (a kind of plastic) and has a matt, or non-shiny, surface.

The bat

There are two main parts of the bat or racket – the blade and the blade covering.

The blade, which includes the handle, is made of wood. The most common blade covering is rubber with a layer of sponge between it and the wood. Different types of rubber are used to help give more speed or spin, or to slow the ball and absorb spin. Some bats have one or two layers of graphite in the wood which help to increase the speed of play.

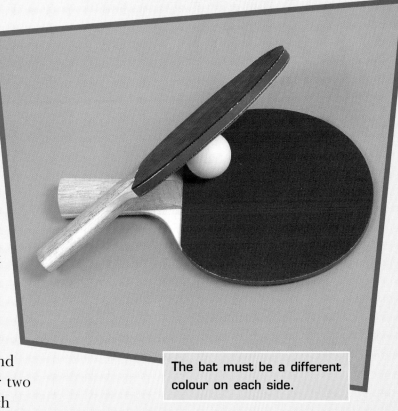

The bat must be a different colour on each side.

Clothing

Comfortable clothing that won't restrict your movement is best. For competitions, players must not wear colours similar to the colour of the ball, as these can make it hard for the opponent to see the ball.

Shoes should be supportive and well cushioned but lightweight enough for fast action.

Skills

Gripping the bat

There are two grips that are commonly used for table tennis – the **shakehand grip** and the **penhold grip**. Try each one and then choose the one you find most comfortable and effective.

The shakehand grip

Take the handle as if you are shaking hands with the bat. Put your index finger across the back of the lower part of the blade. Use your other three fingers and thumb to grip the handle.

The shakehand grip

Forehand shots are played with this side.

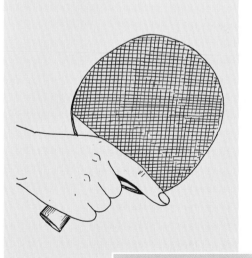

Backhand shots are played with this side.

The shakehand grip will give you good control of the bat.

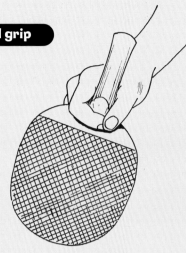

The hitting side.

The penhold grip

Hold the bat around the base of the handle with your thumb and index finger. Your other three fingers curl or spread over the back of the blade.

Using the penhold grip, you hit the ball with the thumb and forefinger side of the bat. Some players occasionally use the other side, but this is very unusual.

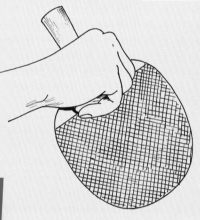

This grip is called the penhold grip because it is similar to the way we hold a pen.

The non-hitting side, fingers curled.

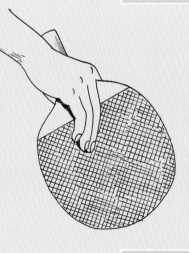

The non-hitting side, fingers straight.

Skills

Your stance

Table tennis is the world's fastest ball game. The ball can travel up to 180 kilometres per hour as it is hit from player to player – that's about 0.1 of a second between hits at top speed!

To play table tennis well you will need to be able to react very quickly. An alert ready position will allow you to move quickly in any direction to hit the ball. Stand slightly to the backhand side of the table, back just far enough so that you could touch the table with the bat if you extended your arm. After each shot, return quickly to the ready position.

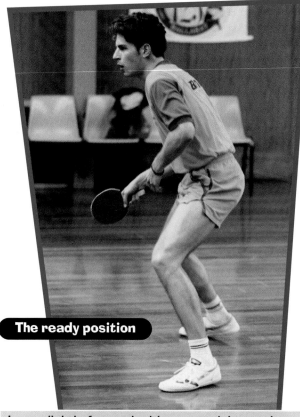

The ready position

Lean slightly forward with your weight on the balls of your feet and your knees bent. Hold your bat at table height in front of your body so that you can move it to either side for a forehand or a backhand shot.

The shuffle step

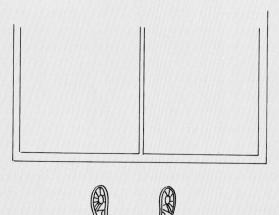

Stand behind the middle line of the table in the ready position.

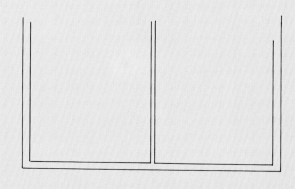

To move right take a short step to the right with your right foot.

Footwork

It is important to be able to move fast in any direction when playing table tennis. Footwork is the key to success and should be practised regularly.

At the beginner level, all footwork involves the **shuffle step**. Even at the elite level, 90 per cent of players' footwork involves the shuffle step.

Once you are sure of the steps, practise them faster with lots of spring from the balls of your feet.

Footwork practice

There are three footwork exercises you can practise with a partner.

1. Ask your partner to hit alternate shots to each side of the table. Use the shuffle step to position yourself to play a backhand and a forehand shot alternately.

2. Ask your partner to hit every shot to your backhand side. Use the shuffle step to position yourself to play a backhand and a forehand shot alternately.

3. Ask your partner to hit two shots to your backhand side and then one to your forehand side and so on. Use the shuffle step to position yourself to play the first ball backhand, the second forehand, and then shuffle wide across the table to hit the third shot forehand and so on.

To move left, follow the same procedure in reverse.

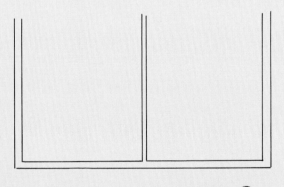

Move your left foot across to your right foot.

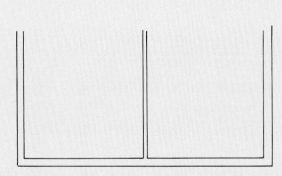

Then move your right foot further right to the ready position.

Skills

The strokes

There are four main strokes that form the basis of other more advanced table tennis shots. It is important to learn each one so that you can play a variety of shots that will be difficult for your opponent to return. You will then be able to return most of your opponent's attacking shots.

The forehand drive

The forehand **drive** is the main attacking shot for many players. It is one of the most powerful shots in the game.

Bring the bat up towards your face as you follow through for the forehand drive. This will allow you to play the shot powerfully and make the ball travel low over the net to bounce on the other side of the table.

Forehand drive

As the ball approaches move from the ready position to stand side-on to the table.

Keep the bat angled slightly downwards as you swing it upwards to hit the ball. Follow through forwards and upwards.

You need it to attack the ball on your forehand side and it can be the shot that wins you the point. Accuracy and speed are important elements of the successful forehand drive.

As the ball approaches your forehand side, move to a position side-on to the table with your feet shoulder-width apart. Hold the bat so that the blade is angled slightly downwards. Extend your arm back to prepare to strike. Hit the ball as it reaches a comfortable height – somewhere between about 10 cm above the table and chest height. Turn your shoulders around to face the table as you play the stroke.

Follow through powerfully, bringing the bat forward as if you are saluting. The ball will travel fast to bounce in the rear half of your opponent's court.

For the backhand drive begin your forwards and upwards follow through as you hit the ball. This will keep the ball low as it travels over the net.

The backhand drive

The backhand drive is used to return shots played to your backhand side of the table. It can be used to force your opponent into making errors.

Most players are naturally weaker at backhand shots – work hard on your backhand otherwise your opponent will always play to your weak side.

Prepare for this stroke by facing the table squarely with your feet shoulder-width apart. This will allow you to react quickly to the left or right to position your body behind the ball. You need to be well balanced on the balls of your feet ready to move in either direction.

Hold the bat in front of your stomach with the blade straight up and down. The action of striking the ball and following through is a little like throwing a frisbee – follow through forwards and upwards so that your arm finishes by pointing in the direction you want the ball to go.

The push

The forehand or the backhand **push** can be used in any sequence of play. The push is usually a safety shot – your aim is to keep the ball in play and avoid losing the point.

The push is usually played against a backspin serve or backspin shot when you don't feel comfortable attacking.

Your aim is to return a difficult ball, but also to prevent your opponent from attacking effectively with the next shot. Keep the ball low, place it well and give it plenty of **backspin** by brushing the bat underneath the ball.

The forehand push

Move into position facing the table. Start the push with the blade of your bat straight up and down. Then as you make contact, brush the bat underneath the ball so that the back of your hand is close to the table and the bat is at an angle of about 45 degrees to the table. Follow through straight towards the net.

As the ball travels over the net, it will dip sharply and bounce upwards forcing your opponent to lunge forwards to reach it.

The forehand push is often played to a short ball. You must move in close to the table for this stroke.

The backhand push

The chop

The **chop**, either forehand or backhand, is an advanced stroke. It is an exaggerated push stroke played from a position well back from the table – usually in response to an opponent's topspin shot. Like the push shots, a chop shot gives the ball backspin.

You can often win with a chop by:
• outlasting your opponent by chopping the ball until he or she returns a bad attacking shot
• forcing an error – play chop shots with varying amounts of spin and kinds of spin so that your opponent misjudges and makes a mistake
• using a chop when your opponent is likely to expect another kind of shot, thereby catching your opponent off guard.

To play the forehand and the backhand chop well you will need a good feel for the ball and fast reactions.

Step back and rotate from the hips so that you are side-on to the table. Contact the ball as it drops from the peak of its bounce with your racket tilted back about 45 degrees. As you hit the ball, follow through downwards and forwards. Return quickly to the ready position for the next stroke.

The backhand push

This shot is similar to the backhand drive – except that you bring the bat under the ball as you hit it.

Begin the stroke with the blade of your bat straight up and down facing the table. As you hit the ball, brush the bat under the ball so that the palm of your hand faces down towards the table. This will give the ball backspin.

Follow through forwards and slightly downwards in the direction you want the ball to travel. As in the forehand push, the ball will dip sharply as it travels over the net.

Skills

The smash

Push forward off your back foot, raise your arm behind the ball and smash it on to your opponent's side of the table.

The block

The **block** is often used to defend an attacking drive. A block can be played when an opponent's strong drive makes a drive return risky.

The block – forehand or backhand – is similar to a drive, however it involves very little backswing and much less follow through. As its name suggests, this shot blocks the path of the ball. If the bat angle is correct the ball will rebound low and fast back over the net to your opponent's side of the table.

You must return quickly to the ready position after playing a block as it is likely that your opponent will return with another attacking shot.

For both the forehand and the backhand block stand close to the table. Move the bat into the path of the ball and hold it so that the blade is angled very slightly downwards. Hit the ball as soon as it has bounced with the centre of the blade. At contact, move the bat forward only slightly.

The smash

The object of the **smash** is to end a rally by hitting the ball as hard as possible so that your opponent has great difficulty in returning it. The smash is usually played with the forehand side. It is the fastest shot in table tennis.

To smash the ball, bring your bat arm straight back in line with the oncoming ball. Strike the ball at the peak of its bounce or, if it is going to bounce higher than eye-level, hit it when it reaches eye-level. As you strike the ball, twist your hips to bring your right shoulder powerfully forward, transferring your weight from your back foot to your front foot. Smash the ball downwards onto your opponent's side of the table. Follow through powerfully, but be careful not to overbalance and (illegally) touch the table or the net.

Practising the smash

When practising the smash, ask your partner to hit the ball to you so that it travels slowly and bounces high. Only play your smashes at full pace when you have mastered the basic technique.

Adding spin

Spin can be added to any shot – increasing your ability to adapt the basic strokes to play a wide variety of shots. A ball with spin is difficult to return so most good players put spin on their shots.

To practise adding spin, ask your partner to hit 'easy' shots to you. Hit the ball with **topspin**, **backspin** or **sidespin**. Until you get used to each one don't worry about whether or not the ball clears the net. When you are more confident, concentrate on placing your shots.

The forehand topspin shot is an exaggerated forehand drive, starting with the bat lower, and turning the body to bring the bat across the ball.

Topspin

Brush the bat across the top of the ball as you hit it – this gives it topspin. As the ball lands its forward spin will drive it low and fast.

Backspin

Brush your bat down and underneath the ball to give it backspin. When it bounces the rebound is slow, forcing your opponent to reach forward.

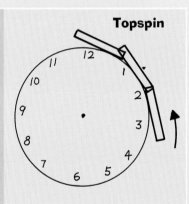

Imagine the ball as the face of a clock. Brush the bat across the ball from the 3 o'clock position to the 12 o'clock position as you hit it. This will give it topspin.

Topspin

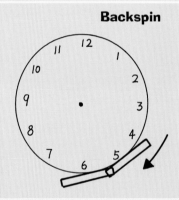

Imagine the ball as the face of a clock. Contact the ball with a brushing action from the 4 o'clock position downwards to the 6 o'clock position. This will give it backspin.

Backspin

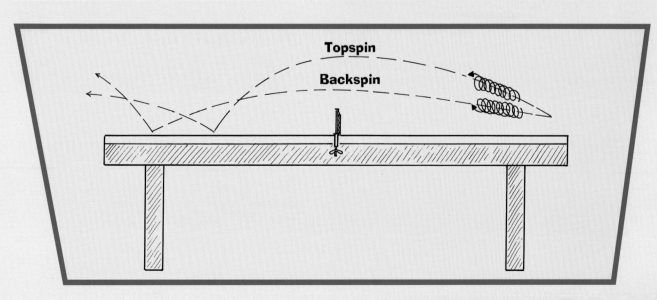

Topspin

Backspin

Serving the ball

Each **rally** begins with a **serve**. If you serve well you will have every chance of controlling the rally and winning the point. By practising a variety of serves, you will be able to start the rally with an attacking shot that your opponent will not be able to predict. You can vary your serves by:

- making some short and some long
- serving long and fast or short and slow
- adding a variety of spin – backspin, topspin, sidespin
- using no spin
- serving forehand or backhand.

The topspin serve can be delivered fast to any part of the table.

Tip

Use the same serving action but change the spin, the speed and the direction of the ball. This will make it hard for your opponent to judge the serve, and the ball will be difficult to return.

There are four serves that you should learn first:

- forehand topspin
- backhand topspin
- forehand backspin
- backhand backspin.

Once you have learned these methods, you will be able to vary your serves. If your opponent is strong against one serve, you'll be able to choose an alternative.

Topspin serves

Topspin serves are the fastest serves and they are ideal when you want to attack from the beginning of the rally. They often force an opponent into a high return which is then easy to attack.

The forehand topspin serve

Hold your bat back from the table with the blade straight up and down. Throw the ball up, and move the bat forwards and upwards with a quick snap action across the ball as you hit it. Keep the ball very low across the net by hitting it when it falls to about net-height.

The ball should bounce first on your side of the table (near your endline) and then land very deep on your opponent's side of the table.

Follow through across your body continuing the up and over motion.

Brush the bat up and over the top of the ball as you hit it.

The backhand topspin serve

The backhand topspin serve has the same effect as the forehand topspin serve but involves a different serving action.

Stand facing the table. Throw the ball up about 50 cm and strike it in front of your body.

Hint

If you want to hit the ball very fast, hit it diagonally across the table. This will give you a greater distance between bounces so that the ball has more space to travel faster and still bounce on the table.

Remember to try to keep your serving action the same whether you are serving diagonally or straight down the table. This will keep your opponent guessing until it is almost too late to prepare a good return.

Brush the bat across the top of the ball as it falls, rolling your wrist slightly so that your knuckles face down to the table as you follow through.

Backspin serves

Backspin serves clear the net low and land short on your opponent's side of the table. After the ball bounces it seems to 'float', hardly travelling forward at all. This forces your opponent to reach forward to hit the ball defensively and should allow you to follow your serve with a strong attacking shot.

Keep your bat almost parallel to the floor, your knees bent, and your eyes fixed on the ball for the forehand backspin serve.

Forehand backspin serve

Stand side-on to the table. Take your bat back so that the blade is nearly parallel to the floor. Throw the ball about 40 cm above table height.

With a forward and slightly downward motion brush the bat under the ball.

Follow through under the ball. It should clear the net low and land short on your opponent's side of the table.

Backhand backspin serve

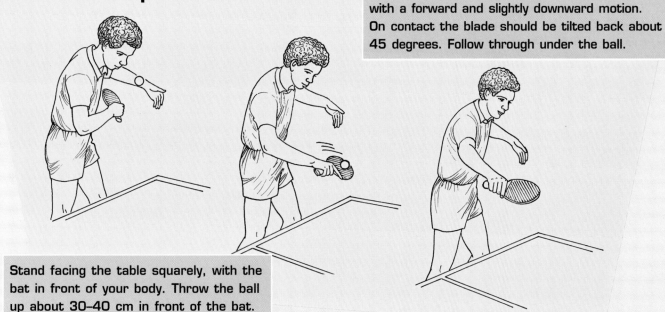

As the ball falls, brush the bat underneath it with a forward and slightly downward motion. On contact the blade should be tilted back about 45 degrees. Follow through under the ball.

Stand facing the table squarely, with the bat in front of your body. Throw the ball up about 30–40 cm in front of the bat.

Sidespin serves

When a ball with sidespin bounces, it accelerates quickly to the left or right. To give a ball sidespin, hit it with the blade of the racket facing upwards using a sharp sideways brushing movement.

Take your bat up and across to your shoulder and throw the ball to about chest height.

Forehand sidespin serve

Throw the ball up to chest height. Strike it with a quick brushing action across the side of the ball.

Backhand sidespin serve

Start this serve from the backhand corner of the table, standing at an angle to the table of about 45 degrees.

Follow through to complete the semi-circular path.

Bring the bat down and across your body in a semi-circular path. As the ball drops to just above table height, brush it in a sideways motion.

Getting ready

The following stretching and strengthening activities will help you to prepare for practice and play.

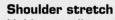

Shoulder stretch
Hold your elbow and pull your arm across your chest until you feel the stretch. Hold the stretch for 30 seconds and then stretch the other side.

Shoulder stretch
Bend your arm behind your head until you feel the stretch. Hold for 30 seconds and then stretch the other side.

Treadmills
Put your hands on the ground shoulder-width apart, and your legs stretched behind you. Bring one foot forwards. Take it back to your starting position and then bring your other foot up. Repeat 10–15 times.

Sit ups
Lie on your back with your knees bent and hands behind your head. Keep your feet flat on the ground and sit up. Repeat 10–15 times.

Arm circles
Stretch your arms up above your head and then take them around in circles. Keep your body upright. Make 10 backward circles and then 10 forward circles.

Side bends
Stand upright. Put one hand on your waist and the other up and over your head. Bend sideways, taking care not to bend forwards. Then stretch the other side.

Sideways jumps
Keep your upper body in the same position and jump your feet about 40 centimetres from side to side, about 10 times.

Taking it further

Addresses

English Table Tennis Association
Queensbury House
Havelock Road
Hastings
East Sussex
TN34 1HF

Scottish Table Tennis Association
Caledonia House
South Gyle
Edinburgh
EA12 9DQ

Table Tennis Association of Wales
31 Maes-y-Celyn
Griffiths Town
Pontypool
Gwent
NT4 5DG

English Schools Table Tennis Association
Mr G Gardniner, General Secretary
36 Froom Street
Chorley
Lancs.
PR6 0AN

(There are secretaries for the ESTTA in most English counties. Ask your sport's teacher or contact the ESTTA General secretary for more information.)

Mrs J Parker MBE
National Coaching Manager
Highfield House
64 Regent Drive
Fulwood
Preston
Lancashire
PR2 3JD

Further reading

ITTF Rules 1995-97, International Table Tennis Federation, London, 1995
Parker, D. & Hewitt, *Playing the Game: Table Tennis*, Ward Lock, London, 1990
Taylor, R. *Action Sports – Table Tennis*, Octopus Books, London, 1989

Glossary

backhand a stroke played across the body. The back of the hand faces the opponent as the ball is hit.

backspin spin given to the ball to make it almost stop travelling forwards after it bounces. The bat is brushed under the ball to give it backspin.

block a quick short stroke without spin, used to return a difficult attacking shot.

chop a low stroke with heavy backspin.

doubles a game of table tennis where two pairs of players compete.

drive an attacking stroke.

forehand a shot played wide of the body with the palm of the playing hand facing the opponent.

game a number of rallies. A game is complete when one player has a score of 21 with a lead of at least two points.

match table tennis is played in matches. A match consists of three or five games.

penhold grip a method of holding the bat, which is similar to the way we hold a pen.

point scoring units. Table tennis is scored in points.

push a stroke with backspin, usually used as a defensive shot.

serve the start of play. The ball is thrown up and hit so that it bounces on the nearside of the table before travelling over the net onto the opponent's half of the table.

shakehand grip a method of holding the bat similar to the the way you would hold a person's hand to shake it.

shuffle step a method of moving from one side of the table to the other to hit the ball.

sidespin spin given to the ball to make it move sideways after it is hit. The bat is brushed across the ball sideways as it is hit.

singles a game of table tennis between two individual players.

smash a hard attacking shot used against a high ball.

topspin spin given to the ball so that it spins forward in its flight and travels low after bouncing. The bat is brushed up and over the ball to give it topspin.

Index